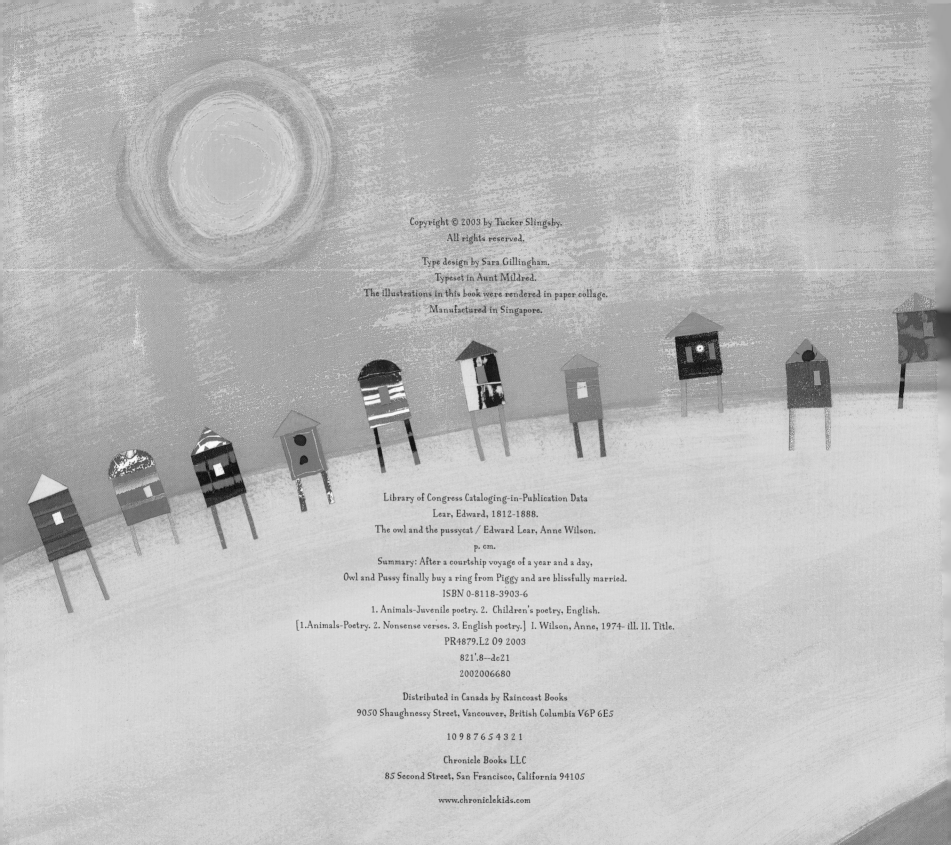

Type design by Sara Gillingham.
Typeset in Aunt Mildred.
The illustrations in this book were rendered in paper collage.
Manufactured in Singapore.

Library of Congress Cataloging-in-Publication Data
Lear, Edward, 1812-1888.
The owl and the pussycat / Edward Lear, Anne Wilson.
p. cm.
Summary: After a courtship voyage of a year and a day,
Owl and Pussy finally buy a ring from Piggy and are blissfully married.
ISBN 0-8118-3903-6
1. Animals-Juvenile poetry. 2. Children's poetry, English.
[1.Animals-Poetry. 2. Nonsense verses. 3. English poetry.] I. Wilson, Anne, 1974- ill. II. Title.
PR4879.L2 O9 2003
821'.8--dc21
2002006680

Distributed in Canada by Raincoast Books
9050 Shaughnessy Street, Vancouver, British Columbia V6P 6E5

10 9 8 7 6 5 4 3 2 1

Chronicle Books LLC
85 Second Street, San Francisco, California 94105

www.chroniclekids.com

The Owl and the Pussycat

BY EDWARD LEAR • ILLUSTRATED BY ANNE WILSON

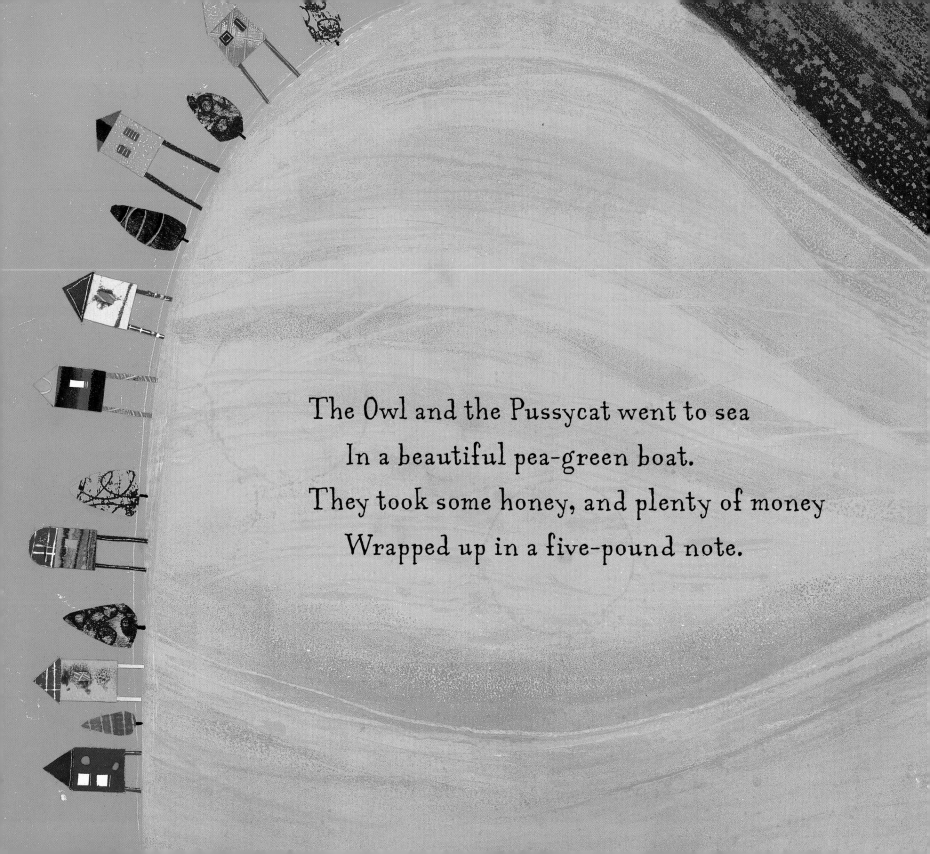

The Owl and the Pussycat went to sea
In a beautiful pea-green boat.
They took some honey, and plenty of money
Wrapped up in a five-pound note.

The Owl looked up
    to the stars above,
    And sang to a small guitar,

"O lovely Pussy! O Pussy, my love,
   What a beautiful Pussy you are,
You are,
   You are!

What a beautiful Pussy you are!"

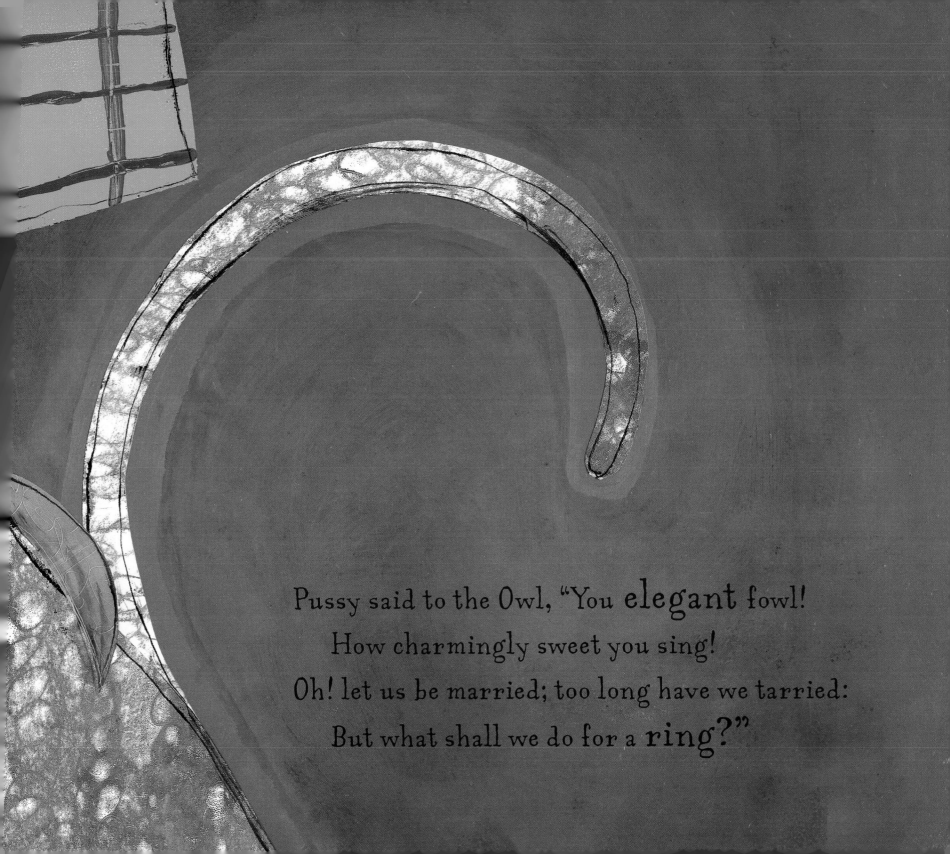

Pussy said to the Owl, "You elegant fowl!

How charmingly sweet you sing!

Oh! let us be married; too long have we tarried:

But what shall we do for a ring?"

They sailed away, for a year and a day,
To the land where the Bong-tree grows,

And there in a wood a Piggy-wig stood,
With a ring at the end of his nose,

His nose,

His nose,

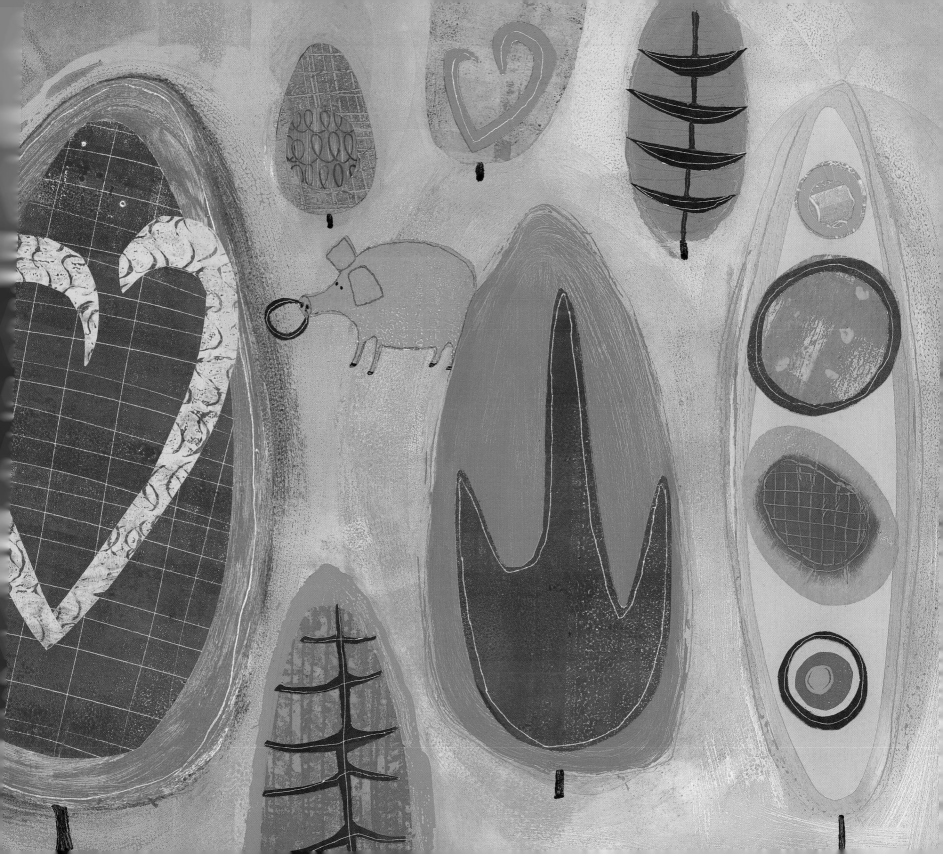

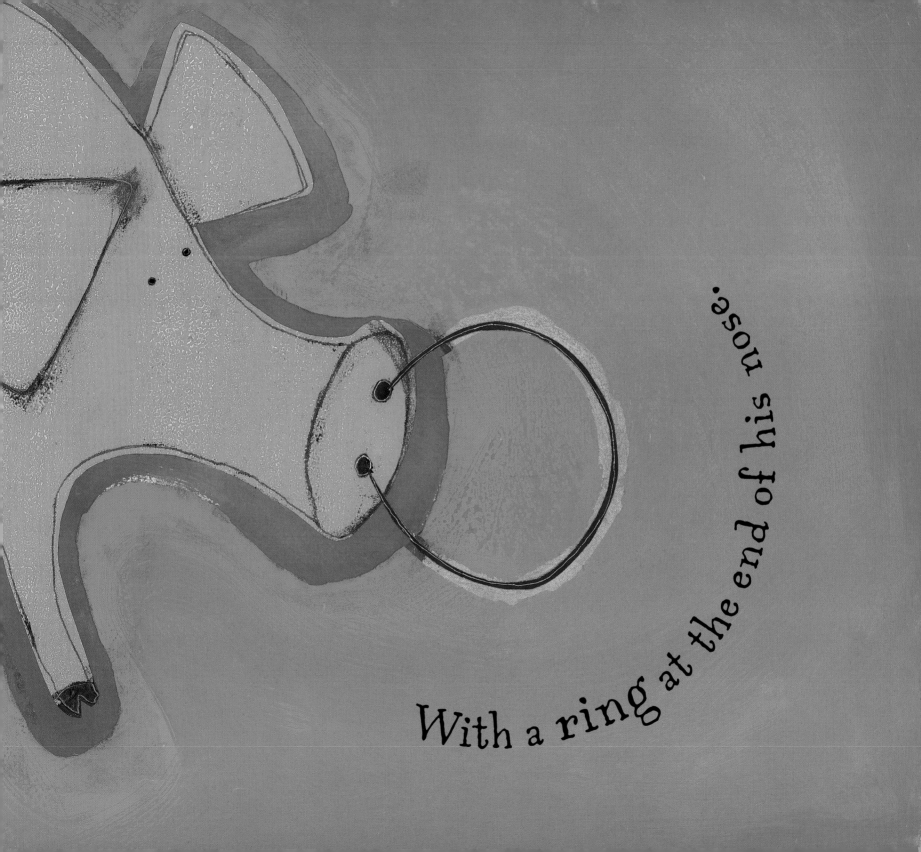

With a ring at the end of his nose.

"Dear Pig, are you willing to sell for one shilling
Your ring?" Said the Piggy, "I will."

So they took it away and were married next day
By the Turkey who lives on the hill.

They dined on mince and slices of quince,

Which they ate with a **runcible spoon**;

And hand in hand, on the edge of the sand,

They danced by the light of the moon,

The moon,

The moon,

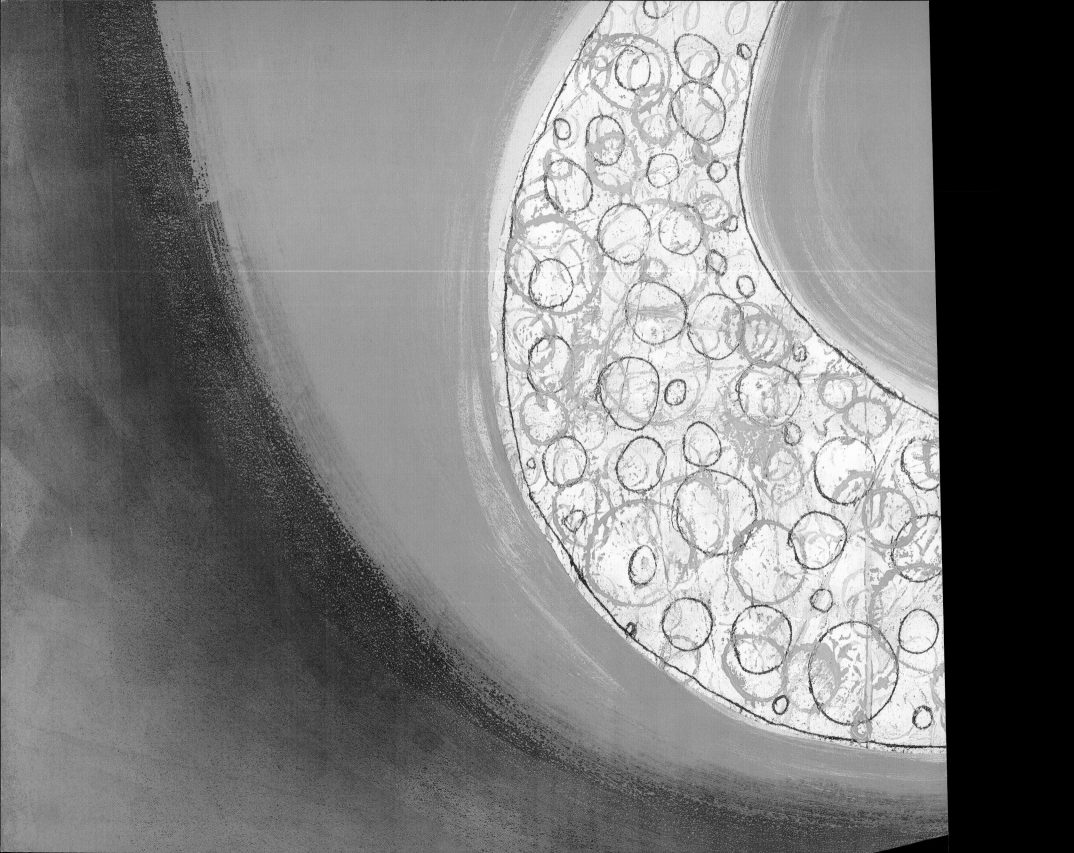

They danced by the light of the moon.